Piercing the Corporate Veil: A Comprehensive Guide for Attorneys

Copyright Page

TITLE: Piercing the Corporate Veil: A Comprehensive Guide for Attorneys

1ST Edition

Copyright @ 2023

ISBN: 9798223481560

Table of Contents

Title Page 1

Piercing the Corporate Veil: A Comprehensive Guide for Attorneys..... 6

Chapter 1: Introduction to Piercing the Corporate Veil 7

Chapter 2: Legal Framework for Piercing the Corporate Veil 14

Chapter 3: Identifying the Grounds for Piercing the Corporate Veil .. 21

Chapter 4: Proving the Elements to Pierce the Corporate Veil.............. 29

Chapter 5: Defending Against Piercing the Corporate Veil Claims..... 37

Chapter 6: Practical Considerations for Attorneys 45

Chapter 7: Jurisdictional Differences in Piercing the Corporate Veil .. 53

Chapter 8: Emerging Trends and Future Developments in Piercing the Corporate Veil 60

Piercing the Corporate Veil: A Comprehensive Guide for Attorneys

By Roberto Miguel Rodriguez

Chapter 1: Introduction to Piercing the Corporate Veil

The Concept of Piercing the Corporate Veil

Piercing the corporate veil is a legal concept that allows courts to hold individual owners of a corporation personally liable for the company's debts and obligations. This concept is of immense importance in the realm of corporate law, and attorneys need to have a comprehensive understanding of it to represent their clients effectively.

In the book "Piercing the Corporate Veil: A Comprehensive Guide for Attorneys," we delve deep into the intricacies of this concept, providing attorneys with a comprehensive resource to navigate the legal considerations associated with piercing the corporate veil.

One of the primary legal considerations discussed in this section is the circumstances under which piercing the corporate veil can be justified. While corporations provide personal liability protection to their owners, there are instances where courts may disregard this protection and hold individuals accountable. We explore the various factors courts consider in such cases, including fraud, undercapitalization, and the failure to observe corporate formalities. By understanding these factors, attorneys can identify situations where piercing the corporate veil could be a viable strategy for their clients.

Furthermore, this section delves into the burden of proof in piercing the corporate veil cases. Attorneys must understand the evidentiary requirements and strategies to demonstrate that the corporate veil should be pierced successfully. We discuss relevant case law and provide practical tips to help attorneys build a compelling case on behalf of their clients.

Additionally, the section addresses the potential defenses against piercing the corporate veil. As attorneys, it is crucial to be aware of the arguments and strategies that can be employed to protect individual owners from personal liability. These defenses could include adequate capitalization, maintaining separate corporate and personal finances, and complying with all corporate formalities.

The section also explores the potential consequences of piercing the corporate veil, both for the individual owners and the corporation itself. Attorneys need to assess the risks and benefits associated with pursuing this legal strategy to provide their clients with informed advice.

By equipping attorneys with a comprehensive understanding of the concept of piercing the corporate veil, this section aims to empower them to effectively represent their clients in cases where individual owners may be held liable for their corporation's debts. With practical insights, case studies, and legal analysis, "Piercing the Corporate Veil: A Comprehensive Guide for Attorneys" serves as an indispensable resource for attorneys navigating the complexities of this legal concept.

Historical Overview of Piercing the Corporate Veil

The concept of piercing the corporate veil is an essential legal consideration in holding individual owners liable for the debts of a corporation. This section provides a historical overview of piercing the corporate veil, tracing its origins and evolution as a legal doctrine.

The idea of a corporate entity separate from its owners has existed for centuries, dating back to the Roman Empire. However, it was only during the industrial revolution in the late 19th century that corporations began to play a significant role in economic development. As corporations grew in size and influence, the need for a legal framework to govern their actions became apparent.

The corporate veil, which refers to the legal separation between a corporation and its owners, was first challenged in the landmark case of Salomon v. Salomon & Co. Ltd. in 1897. In this case, the House of Lords in the United Kingdom held that a corporation is a distinct legal entity separate from its shareholders. This decision established the principle of limited liability, shielding shareholders from personal liability for the debts of the corporation.

However, as corporations gained more power and influence, concerns arose regarding their potential abuse and evasion of legal obligations. This led to the development of the doctrine of piercing the corporate veil. The doctrine allows a court to disregard the corporate entity and hold individual owners personally liable for the corporation's debts in certain circumstances.

Over the years, courts have developed various tests and factors to determine when piercing the corporate veil is appropriate. These include inadequate capitalization, commingling of assets, fraud, and using the corporate entity to perpetrate injustice or fraud.

The historical overview of piercing the corporate veil also includes an examination of critical cases that have shaped the doctrine. These cases, such as Walkovszky v. Carlton and Sea-Land Services, Inc. v. Pepper Source, Ltd., provide valuable insights into the application and limitations of piercing the corporate veil.

As attorneys, understanding the historical development of piercing the corporate veil is crucial for navigating the complexities of holding individual owners liable for corporate debts. By delving into the origins and evolution of this doctrine, attorneys can effectively advocate for their clients and ensure justice is served in cases where the corporate veil needs to be pierced.

In conclusion, this section provides attorneys with a comprehensive historical overview of piercing the corporate veil. By exploring the origins, evolution, and critical cases, attorneys can gain a deep understanding of this crucial legal doctrine and its application in holding individual owners liable for corporate debts.

Importance of Piercing the Corporate Veil in Debt Recovery

Introduction:

When it comes to debt recovery, it is not uncommon for some corporate entities to use the concept of the "corporate veil" as a shield to protect their owners from personal liability. However, understanding the importance of piercing the corporate veil can be crucial in ensuring that justice is served and debts are recovered. This section will explore the legal considerations in piercing the corporate veil to hold individual owners liable for debts, providing attorneys with a comprehensive guide on this topic.

Understanding the Corporate Veil:

The corporate veil refers to the legal concept that separates a corporation from its owners, protecting them from personal liability for the company's debts. While this veil is essential for encouraging entrepreneurship and investment, it can also be misused to evade financial obligations. Attorneys play a vital role in piercing this veil to hold the responsible parties accountable.

Legal Considerations:

1. Alter Ego Doctrine: Attorneys need to ronderstand the legal principles of the alter ego doctrine, which allows a court to disregard the corporate entity and hold individual owners personally liable for the company's debts. This doctrine is typically applied when there is evidence of misuse

or abuse of the corporate form, such as commingling of funds or failure to maintain corporate formalities.

2. Fraudulent Conveyance: Debtors often attempt to transfer assets to related entities or individuals to avoid creditors. Attorneys must be familiar with the laws governing fraudulent conveyance, which enable them to challenge such transactions and ensure that the assets are available for debt recovery.

3. Undercapitalization: Many corporations intentionally maintain insufficient capitalization, making it difficult for creditors to recover their debts. Attorneys must be skilled in identifying cases of undercapitalization and proving that it was done with the intent to defraud creditors, thereby piercing the corporate veil.

4. Piercing for Group Liability: In certain situations, individual owners can be held liable for the debts of a group of related corporations. Attorneys should understand the legal grounds for piercing the corporate veil to extend liability beyond a single entity and recover debts from multiple sources.

Conclusion:

For attorneys involved in debt recovery, understanding the importance of piercing the corporate veil is paramount. By familiarizing themselves with the legal considerations discussed in this section, attorneys can effectively navigate the complexities of holding individual owners liable for corporate debts. By piercing the corporate veil, attorneys play a crucial role in upholding justice and ensuring that debtors are held accountable for their financial obligations.

Challenges and Controversies Surrounding Piercing the Corporate Veil

Piercing the corporate veil is a legal doctrine that holds the potential to expose individual owners of a corporation to personal liability for the debts and obligations of the business entity. While this concept serves as a crucial tool in ensuring accountability and preventing misuse of the corporate form, it is not without its challenges and controversies. In this section, we will delve into the intricacies and complexities surrounding piercing the corporate veil, providing attorneys with a comprehensive understanding of the subject matter.

One of the primary challenges attorneys face when considering piercing the corporate veil is establishing the necessary legal grounds. Courts typically require a showing of fraud, injustice, or other compelling circumstances to warrant the disregard of corporate separateness. This burden of proof can be demanding, as attorneys must navigate through a multitude of factors, including inadequate capitalization, commingling of funds, and failure to follow corporate formalities. Understanding the intricacies of each factor and how they interrelate is crucial for attorneys seeking to pierce the corporate veil successfully.

Another area of contention revolves around the differing standards applied by courts across jurisdictions. While some jurisdictions adopt a more lenient approach, others are more stringent, making it challenging for attorneys to predict the outcome of their cases. Furthermore, the lack of a uniform legal framework and the absence of explicit statutory guidelines contribute to the controversy surrounding piercing the corporate veil.

Additionally, attorneys must be aware of the potential backlash from opposing parties and the corporate community. When piercing the corporate veil, they may encounter resistance from both the corporation and its owners, who are likely to defend against personal liability vigorously. Moreover, this practice can create uncertainty and disrupt the stability of the corporate form, leading to concerns among businesses and entrepreneurs.

Despite these challenges and controversies, piercing the corporate veil remains a vital legal consideration for attorneys. Understanding the limitations and potential pitfalls associated with this doctrine is imperative to effectively navigate the complexities of holding individual owners liable for corporate debts. By staying abreast of developments in case law and maintaining a comprehensive understanding of the factors involved, attorneys can provide their clients with sound advice and representation in this intricate area of law.

In conclusion, this section serves as a comprehensive guide for attorneys, offering an in-depth exploration of the challenges and controversies surrounding piercing the corporate veil. By providing clarity on legal considerations, jurisdictional disparities, and potential backlash, attorneys can enhance their understanding of this complex subject matter, enabling them to effectively advocate for their clients in holding individual owners liable for corporate debts.

Chapter 2: Legal Framework for Piercing the Corporate Veil

Statutory Provisions for Piercing the Corporate Veil

In the realm of corporate law, the concept of the corporate veil is essential to understanding the separation between a corporation and its owners. However, there are instances where this veil can be pierced, allowing creditors to hold individual owners personally liable for the debts of the corporation. This section will delve into the statutory provisions surrounding this legal consideration and provide attorneys with a comprehensive guide to navigating the complexities of piercing the corporate veil.

One of the critical statutes that attorneys must be familiar with is the Uniform Fraudulent Transfer Act (UFTA). Under the UFTA, a court may disregard the corporate entity and hold individual owners liable if they have fraudulently transferred assets to avoid paying debts. Attorneys must be well-versed in the various factors that courts consider when determining whether a fraudulent transfer has occurred, such as the intent to hinder, delay, or defraud creditors.

Another necessary statutory provision is the Uniform Commercial Code (UCC). Attorneys need to understand the UCC's provisions regarding the personal liability of individual owners in situations where they have personally guaranteed the debts of the corporation. This section will delve into the intricacies of UCC provisions and provide attorneys with the necessary tools to effectively argue for the piercing of the corporate veil based on personal guarantees.

Furthermore, attorneys must also familiarize themselves with state-specific statutory provisions that govern the piercing of the corporate veil. Each state has its own set of laws and regulations that determine when and how the corporate veil can be pierced. This section will provide an overview of some of the standard statutory provisions across different states, highlighting key differences and essential considerations.

Understanding the statutory provisions for piercing the corporate veil is crucial for attorneys representing both creditors seeking to hold individual owners personally liable and individual owners seeking to protect themselves from such liability. By providing a comprehensive guide to these provisions, this section aims to equip attorneys with the knowledge and tools they need to navigate the legal considerations surrounding piercing the corporate veil effectively.

In conclusion, this section will explore the statutory provisions governing the piercing of the corporate veil. Attorneys will gain a thorough understanding of the Uniform Fraudulent Transfer Act, the Uniform Commercial Code, and state-specific laws, empowering them to effectively advocate for their clients' interests in cases involving personal liability for corporate debts. With this comprehensive guide in hand, attorneys will be well-prepared to navigate the intricacies of piercing the corporate veil and achieve favorable outcomes for their clients.

Common Law Principles for Piercing the Corporate Veil

Introduction:

In the legal world, the concept of piercing the corporate veil refers to a situation where the courts disregard the legal entity of a corporation and hold individual owners personally liable for the company's debts or actions. This section aims to provide attorneys with a comprehensive understanding of the common law principles governing the piercing of the corporate veil. By delving into these principles, attorneys can navigate the complexities of this legal strategy and effectively advocate for their clients.

Understanding the Corporate Veil:

Before delving into the common law principles, it is crucial to grasp the concept of the corporate veil. Corporations are separate legal entities, distinct from their owners. The corporate veil acts as a shield, protecting shareholders and directors from personal liability for the company's obligations. However, there are situations where this veil can be pierced, allowing creditors or claimants to reach the personal assets of the owners.

Common Law Principles:

1. Fraud or Improper Conduct: Courts are more likely to pierce the corporate veil when there is evidence of fraud, improper conduct, or injustice. If the corporate form is used to perpetrate fraud or shield illegal activities, the courts may disregard the corporate entity and hold the individuals accountable.

2. Undercapitalization: Inadequate capitalization is another factor that courts consider when piercing the corporate veil. If the owners fail to provide sufficient capital to run the business or maintain appropriate reserves, the courts may hold them personally liable for the debts incurred.

3. Alter Ego Doctrine: The alter ego doctrine allows the courts to pierce the corporate veil when the owners treat the corporation as an extension of themselves rather than a separate entity. This occurs when there is a lack of separation between personal and corporate finances, misuse of corporate assets, or failure to follow corporate formalities.

4. Unjust Enrichment: If the owners have unfairly benefited from the corporate structure at the expense of creditors or claimants, the courts may pierce the corporate veil to prevent unjust enrichment.

Conclusion:

Understanding the common law principles for piercing the corporate veil is vital for attorneys dealing with legal considerations in holding individual owners liable for corporate debts. By recognizing these principles, attorneys can effectively argue their cases and navigate the complexities of corporate law. However, it is crucial to analyze each case independently, considering the specific circumstances and jurisdictional variations when determining whether the corporate veil should be pierced.

Factors Considered by Courts in Piercing the Corporate Veil

In the realm of corporate law, the concept of piercing the corporate veil is a crucial tool that attorneys can employ to hold individual owners liable for the debts of a corporation. This legal doctrine allows courts to disregard the limited liability protection typically afforded to shareholders, thus exposing them to personal liability for the corporation's obligations. However, courts only resort to piercing the corporate veil under specific circumstances, considering a range of factors to ensure that it is an equitable and just remedy.

One primary factor that courts assess is the level of control exercised by the individual owners over the corporation. Suppose the owners have complete domination and control over the corporation, using it as a mere instrumentality to conduct personal affairs or commit fraud. In that case, courts may be inclined to pierce the corporate veil. This factor is particularly relevant when owners commingle personal and corporate funds, disregard corporate formalities, or fail to maintain adequate records and accounts.

Another factor courts consider is whether the corporation was adequately capitalized at the time of its formation. Insufficient capitalization can be indicative of an intent to defraud creditors or an inability to meet financial obligations. If owners intentionally undercapitalize the corporation, courts may hold them personally liable for the corporation's debts.

Courts also examine whether the corporation is being used to perpetrate fraud or injustice. Suppose the owners utilize the corporate entity to shield themselves from personal liability while engaging in wrongful conduct, such as fraudulent activities or intentional harm to creditors. In that case, courts may pierce the corporate veil to prevent the abuse and ensure that justice is served.

Furthermore, courts consider whether adherence to the principle of limited liability would result in an unfair or inequitable outcome. If allowing shareholders to escape personal liability would unjustly deprive an innocent party of a remedy, courts may disregard the corporate entity and hold individual owners accountable.

Attorneys need to understand these factors and present compelling arguments that demonstrate the existence of one or more of them when seeking to pierce the corporate veil. Convincing courts to pierce the corporate veil requires a thorough examination of the specific circumstances surrounding the corporation and its owners.

In conclusion, piercing the corporate veil is a robust legal doctrine that allows courts to hold individual owners personally liable for a corporation's debts. However, courts carefully consider various factors such as control, capitalization, fraud, and equity before resorting to this remedy. Attorneys must be well-versed in these factors and effectively present their arguments to pierce the corporate veil and ensure justice is served successfully.

Case Studies on Successful and Unsuccessful Attempts to Pierce the Corporate Veil

Introduction:

In the realm of corporate law, the concept of piercing the corporate veil is a powerful tool that allows courts to hold individual owners personally liable for the debts and obligations of their businesses. However, successfully piercing the corporate veil requires a deep understanding of legal considerations and a careful analysis of the specific circumstances involved. This section explores a series of case studies, highlighting both successful and unsuccessful attempts to pierce the corporate veil, providing valuable insights for attorneys navigating this complex area of law.

Case Study 1: Successful Piercing of the Corporate Veil:

In this case, a small construction company was found liable for environmental damages caused by its operations. The court successfully pierced the corporate veil and held the individual owners personally responsible for the company's debts. The key factors that led to this outcome were the owners' commingling of personal and company funds, failure to maintain proper corporate formalities and use of the company as a mere alter ego for personal gain. This case illustrates the importance of maintaining a clear separation between personal and corporate finances, as well as adhering to corporate formalities.

Case Study 2: Unsuccessful Attempt to Pierce the Corporate Veil:

In this instance, a group of investors sought to hold the individual owners of a startup technology firm personally liable for the company's failure to deliver on promised services. However, the court rejected the piercing of the corporate veil argument, citing that the owners had indeed maintained proper corporate formalities, had separate bank accounts, and had not engaged in any fraudulent activities. This case emphasizes the significance of demonstrating clear evidence of disregard for corporate formalities or fraudulent behavior when attempting to pierce the corporate veil.

Case Study 3: The Role of Alter Ego Doctrine:

In this case, a large manufacturing corporation attempted to escape liability for an environmental disaster by creating a subsidiary solely for that specific operation. The subsidiary lacked sufficient capital and resources to handle potential liabilities. The court pierced the corporate veil, applying the alter ego doctrine, as the subsidiary was found to be a mere instrumentality of the parent company. This case demonstrates how the alter ego doctrine can be an effective tool to hold parent companies accountable for the actions of their subsidiaries.

Conclusion:

These case studies provide attorneys with valuable insights into the legal considerations involved in piercing the corporate veil. They underscore the importance of maintaining a clear separation between personal and corporate finances, adhering to corporate formalities, and demonstrating evidence of disregard for proper corporate structure or fraudulent behavior. By understanding the nuances of successful and unsuccessful attempts to pierce the corporate veil, attorneys can effectively guide their clients through this complex area of law, ensuring fair outcomes and protecting their client's interests.

Chapter 3: Identifying the Grounds for Piercing the Corporate Veil

Alter Ego Doctrine: Determining When the Corporate Entity is an Alter Ego

The Alter Ego Doctrine is a legal principle that allows courts to disregard the separate legal entity of a corporation and hold individual owners personally liable for the corporation's debts or actions. This doctrine is often invoked in cases where the corporate veil is pierced, meaning that the court finds that the corporate entity is being used as a mere facade or alter ego for the individual owners.

For attorneys dealing with legal considerations in piercing the corporate veil to hold individual owners liable for debts, understanding when the Alter Ego Doctrine applies is crucial. This section aims to provide a comprehensive guide to help attorneys navigate this complex legal terrain.

Determining whether the corporate entity is an alter ego requires a careful analysis of several factors. Courts typically consider factors such as the commingling of funds, failure to follow corporate formalities, inadequate capitalization, and the overall control exerted by individual owners over the corporation. However, it is essential to note that the presence of one or two factors alone may not be sufficient to establish alter ego liability. Instead, a holistic approach is taken, considering the totality of the circumstances.

One key factor in determining an alter ego is the commingling of funds. If personal and corporate funds are consistently mixed, or if the corporation is used as a personal piggy bank by the owners, courts may find that the corporate entity is merely an alter ego for the individual owners.

Another factor is the failure to follow corporate formalities. This includes disregarding corporate bylaws, holding irregular or undocumented meetings, and failing to maintain proper corporate records. Such disregard for corporate formalities can indicate that the corporation is being used as an alter ego for personal purposes.

Inadequate capitalization is also a significant factor. Suppose the corporation is undercapitalized and cannot reasonably cover potential liabilities. In that case, it may suggest that the corporate entity is a mere facade, and the individual owners should be held liable.

Finally, courts will consider the overall control exerted by individual owners over the corporation. If the owners exercise complete domination and control over the corporation, making all major decisions without regard for corporate formalities or the best interests of the corporation, alter ego liability may be imposed.

Attorneys representing clients seeking to pierce the corporate veil should be well-versed in these factors and understand how to build a strong case. By presenting evidence that convincingly demonstrates the presence of alter ego factors, attorneys can successfully argue for the personal liability of individual owners.

In conclusion, the Alter Ego Doctrine provides a crucial tool for attorneys dealing with legal considerations in piercing the corporate veil. By thoroughly evaluating factors such as commingling of funds, failure to follow corporate formalities, inadequate capitalization, and overall control, attorneys can effectively determine when the corporate entity is an alter ego. This section aims to equip attorneys with the knowledge and strategies necessary to navigate this complex area of law and achieve successful outcomes for their clients.

Fraudulent or Improper Use of Corporate Structure

In the legal realm, the concept of piercing the corporate veil refers to a legal action that allows individuals to hold corporate owners personally liable for the debts and obligations of the corporation. This section explores the specific legal considerations surrounding the fraudulent or improper use of corporate structure, shedding light on the circumstances under which the corporate veil can be pierced.

Attorneys specializing in corporate law have a crucial role in guiding clients through the complex terrain of corporate structures and ensuring compliance with legal requirements. Understanding the fraudulent or improper use of corporate structure is essential in protecting the interests of both corporations and their stakeholders.

The section begins by delving into the concept of fraudulent or improper use of corporate structure. It explores instances where individuals may manipulate the corporate form to shield themselves from personal liability, such as asset transfers, undercapitalization, and commingling of funds. By analyzing case law precedents, this section provides attorneys with a comprehensive overview of the various tactics employed by individuals attempting to defraud creditors or avoid legal obligations.

Next, the section delves into the legal considerations when attempting to pierce the corporate veil. Attorneys must navigate a myriad of factors, such as demonstrating fraud, alter ego or inadequate capitalization. This section provides in-depth analysis and practical examples to assist attorneys in building strong cases for piercing the corporate veil.

Moreover, the section addresses the burden of proof required to pierce the corporate veil successfully. Attorneys will find valuable insights regarding the evidence necessary to establish fraudulent or improper use of corporate structure, including financial records, corporate governance documents, and witness testimonies. This section also explores the importance of conducting thorough investigations and due diligence to uncover hidden assets or fraudulent activities.

Lastly, the section offers practical recommendations and strategies for attorneys representing either the plaintiff or the defendant in piercing the corporate veil cases. It discusses settlement negotiations, alternative dispute resolution methods, and the potential impact of piercing the corporate veil on corporate governance and liability.

Overall, this section provides attorneys with a comprehensive understanding of the fraudulent or improper use of corporate structure and the legal considerations involved in piercing the corporate veil. By equipping attorneys with the necessary knowledge and tools, this section empowers them to effectively navigate these complex legal issues and protect the interests of their clients.

Undercapitalization and Failure to Maintain Corporate Formalities

One of the most important legal considerations in piercing the corporate veil to hold individual owners liable for debts is the issue of undercapitalization and failure to maintain corporate formalities. This section delves into the significance of these factors and how they can impact the ability to pierce the corporate veil.

Undercapitalization refers to a situation where a corporation lacks sufficient funds and resources to meet its financial obligations. When a corporation is undercapitalized, it becomes more likely that its owners will be held personally liable for the company's debts. This is because the courts may view undercapitalization as evidence that the corporation is merely an alter ego of its owners rather than a separate legal entity. As a result, the courts may decide to "pierce the corporate veil" and hold the owners personally liable for the corporation's debts.

Maintaining corporate formalities is another crucial aspect in determining whether the corporate veil can be pierced. Corporate formalities include adhering to proper procedures for holding meetings, keeping accurate records, and maintaining a clear separation between the corporation and its owners. Failure to observe these formalities can weaken the legal distinction between the corporation and its owners, making it easier for the courts to hold the owners personally liable.

This section explores various scenarios where undercapitalization and failure to maintain corporate formalities can lead to piercing the corporate veil. It provides an in-depth analysis of relevant case law, highlighting key factors that courts consider when evaluating these issues. Additionally, it offers practical guidance for attorneys representing clients who may be facing potential liability due to these factors.

Attorneys will find this section to be an invaluable resource in understanding the legal considerations involved in piercing the corporate veil. By examining real-world examples and analyzing the legal principles at play, attorneys can develop effective strategies to protect their client's interests and minimize potential liability. Furthermore, this section sheds light on the importance of proper capitalization and corporate formalities, emphasizing the need for diligent compliance to maintain the legal protection afforded by the corporate entity.

In conclusion, undercapitalization and failure to maintain corporate formalities are critical factors that can influence the court's decision to pierce the corporate veil. Attorneys must be well-versed in these issues to effectively represent their clients and navigate the complexities of corporate liability. This section offers comprehensive insights and practical guidance to help attorneys understand and navigate the legal landscape surrounding piercing the corporate veil.

Avoidance of Legal Obligations through the Corporate Veil

One of the most common challenges attorneys face when dealing with corporate entities is the issue of avoiding legal obligations through the corporate veil. Many entities use the corporate structure to shield their owners from personal liability for the debts and obligations of the company. However, in certain circumstances, it becomes necessary to pierce this corporate veil and hold the individual owners liable for the company's debts. This section aims to provide attorneys with a comprehensive guide on legal considerations in piercing the corporate veil.

Piercing the corporate veil is a legal concept that allows courts to disregard the separate legal personality of a corporation and hold its shareholders or owners personally liable for the company's actions or debts. This doctrine is invoked when the corporate structure is abused, and it becomes necessary to prevent injustice or fraud.

Attorneys need to be familiar with various legal considerations when attempting to pierce the corporate veil. Firstly, they must establish that the company is a mere alter ego or an extension of its owners rather than an independent legal entity. This involves demonstrating that the owners commingle personal and corporate funds, fail to observe corporate formalities or use the company as a mere shell to conduct personal business.

Another important consideration is the existence of fraudulent intent. If the corporate structure was deliberately used to defraud creditors or evade legal obligations, courts are more likely to pierce the corporate veil. Attorneys must provide evidence of fraudulent conduct, such as diversion of assets, intentional misrepresentation, or the absence of legitimate business purpose.

Additionally, attorneys should be aware of the specific legal requirements and standards set by their jurisdiction for piercing the corporate veil. Different states may have different tests or factors that need to be satisfied before the court can disregard the corporate entity. It is crucial to understand these requirements and tailor the legal strategy accordingly.

Furthermore, attorneys should be prepared to address potential defenses raised by the opposing party. These may include arguments regarding limited liability, lack of personal benefit, or the importance of preserving the corporate structure. Appropriate counterarguments and evidence must be presented to overcome these defenses effectively.

In conclusion, the avoidance of legal obligations through the corporate veil is a complex issue that requires careful consideration. Attorneys must be well-versed in the legal considerations involved in piercing the corporate veil to hold individual owners liable for their company's debts effectively. By understanding the elements necessary to establish alter ego liability, fraudulent intent, jurisdiction-specific requirements, and potential defenses, attorneys can navigate this challenging area of law and protect the rights of their clients.

Piercing the Corporate Veil in Parent-Subsidiary Relationships

Introduction:

In the complex world of corporate law, parent-subsidiary relationships can often present unique challenges. One such challenge is the concept of piercing the corporate veil, which allows for individual owners to be held personally liable for the debts of their corporation. This section aims to provide attorneys with a comprehensive guide on the legal considerations involved in piercing the corporate veil in parent-subsidiary relationships.

Understanding Parent-Subsidiary Relationships:

Before delving into the intricacies of piercing the corporate veil, it is crucial to grasp the nature of parent-subsidiary relationships. A subsidiary is a distinct legal entity separate from its parent company. However, under certain circumstances, the corporate veil that separates the parent and subsidiary can be pierced, leading to the imposition of personal liability on individual owners.

Factors for Piercing the Corporate Veil:

Attorneys must be well-versed in the factors that courts consider when determining whether to pierce the corporate veil in parent-subsidiary relationships. These factors often include inadequate capitalization, commingling of assets, failure to observe corporate formalities, and using the subsidiary to perpetrate fraud. Understanding these factors is essential to build a strong case for piercing the corporate veil.

Legal Precedents and Case Studies:

To provide attorneys with practical insights, this section will highlight prominent legal precedents and case studies where courts have pierced the corporate veil in parent-subsidiary relationships. Through these examples, attorneys can glean valuable lessons and strategies for their cases.

Best Practices and Risk Mitigation:

As attorneys, it is crucial to help clients navigate the potential risks associated with parent-subsidiary relationships. This section will offer best practices and risk mitigation strategies to corporate clients to avoid piercing the corporate veil. By implementing these practices, attorneys can help clients safeguard their assets and limit their exposure to liability.

Conclusion:

Piercing the corporate veil in parent-subsidiary relationships is a complex legal concept that requires a deep understanding of corporate law and a keen eye for detail. This section has provided attorneys with a comprehensive guide on the legal considerations involved in piercing the corporate veil in parent-subsidiary relationships. By equipping attorneys with practical insights, legal precedents, and risk mitigation strategies, they can better serve their clients and navigate the intricate world of corporate law.

Chapter 4: Proving the Elements to Pierce the Corporate Veil

Gathering Sufficient Evidence to Establish Alter Ego Liability

In the realm of corporate law, piercing the corporate veil is a legal concept that allows individuals to hold the owners or shareholders of a corporation personally liable for the company's debts or actions. This concept, known as alter ego liability, is particularly important when dealing with cases where a corporation is being used as a shield to perpetrate fraud or injustice. For attorneys navigating the complex world of corporate law, understanding the process of gathering sufficient evidence to establish alter ego liability is crucial.

To successfully establish alter ego liability, attorneys must present compelling evidence to demonstrate that the corporation is nothing more than a mere instrumentality or alter ego of its owners. This usually involves proving that the owners have disregarded the corporate formalities and have treated the business as an extension of themselves rather than as a separate legal entity.

One key aspect of gathering evidence is to examine the financial transactions between the corporation and its owners. Attorneys should meticulously review bank records, financial statements, and tax returns to identify any commingling of funds or personal use of corporate assets by the owners. Inconsistencies in financial records, such as personal expenses being paid directly from the corporate account, can strengthen the argument for alter ego liability.

Furthermore, attorneys should delve into the decision-making process within the corporation. Evidence that the owners have complete control over the company's operations, without any meaningful input from other shareholders or directors, can help establish alter ego liability. This can be demonstrated through written agreements, meeting minutes, or witness testimonies.

Another vital aspect is scrutinizing the corporate structure and formalities. Attorneys should examine whether the corporation has followed necessary legal requirements, such as holding regular shareholder meetings, keeping proper corporate records, and adhering to corporate bylaws. Any failure to comply with these formalities can be used to support the argument that the owners have treated the corporation as their alter ego.

To bolster the case for alter ego liability, attorneys should also investigate the level of capitalization in the corporation. Insufficient capitalization, where the owners have not adequately funded the business, can indicate that the corporation was never intended to operate as a separate entity. By demonstrating that the owners have failed to maintain proper financial support for the corporation, attorneys can strengthen the argument for alter ego liability.

In conclusion, gathering sufficient evidence to establish alter ego liability is a critical step in piercing the corporate veil and holding individual owners liable for a corporation's debts. By carefully examining financial transactions, decision-making processes, corporate formalities, and capitalization levels, attorneys can build a persuasive case to demonstrate that the corporation is nothing more than an alter ego of its owners. With a comprehensive understanding of the evidentiary requirements, attorneys can effectively navigate the complexities of alter ego liability and seek justice for their clients.

Demonstrating Fraudulent or Improper Use of the Corporate Structure

The corporate structure acts as a shield that protects individual owners from personal liability for the debts and obligations of their company. However, there are instances where the corporate veil can be pierced, allowing creditors to hold individual owners accountable. This section aims to provide attorneys with a comprehensive guide on the legal considerations involved in piercing the corporate veil to hold individual owners liable for debts.

One of the critical factors in successfully piercing the corporate veil is demonstrating fraudulent or improper use of the corporate structure. Attorneys must understand the various indicators that can help establish such misuse. These indicators may include commingling of funds, inadequate capitalization, failure to maintain corporate formalities and diversion of assets.

Commingling of funds refers to the mixing of personal and corporate funds, which is a clear violation of the corporate structure. Attorneys need to gather evidence showcasing instances where owners used company funds for personal expenses or vice versa. Such evidence can significantly strengthen the argument for piercing the corporate veil.

Inadequate capitalization is another critical consideration. Attorneys must analyze whether the corporation was initially capitalized with enough funds to cover its potential liabilities reasonably. Insufficient capitalization can be a sign that the owners intended to defraud creditors from the outset.

Failure to maintain corporate formalities can also be indicative of fraudulent or improper use of the corporate structure. Attorneys should investigate whether the company adhered to corporate governance requirements, such as holding regular board meetings, maintaining accurate records, and filing required reports. Any failure to comply with these formalities can undermine the separation between the owners and the corporation, making it easier to pierce the corporate veil.

Lastly, attorneys should explore instances of asset diversion, where owners intentionally transfer company assets to themselves or other entities to hinder creditor claims. This could involve fraudulent transfers or sham transactions that aim to deplete the company's assets and leave creditors with nothing.

By thoroughly examining and presenting evidence of fraudulent or improper use of the corporate structure, attorneys can build a strong case for piercing the corporate veil. It is crucial to remember that each case will present unique challenges, requiring attorneys to analyze and apply relevant legal principles carefully. With a comprehensive understanding of legal considerations in piercing the corporate veil, attorneys can effectively advocate for their clients and hold individual owners liable for corporate debts.

Establishing Undercapitalization and Failure to Observe Corporate Formalities

In the legal world, the concept of piercing the corporate veil has become increasingly significant when it comes to holding individual owners liable for the debts of their corporations. This section aims to provide attorneys with a comprehensive guide on two crucial aspects that can contribute to piercing the corporate veil: undercapitalization and failure to observe corporate formalities.

Undercapitalization refers to the situation where a corporation lacks sufficient funds or assets to meet its obligations. When a corporation is undercapitalized, it becomes vulnerable to claims by creditors seeking to hold individual owners personally liable for the company's debts. Attorneys need to understand the elements required to establish undercapitalization and effectively argue their case to hold the owners accountable.

To prove undercapitalization, attorneys must demonstrate that the corporation failed to maintain adequate capital at the time of its formation or during its operation. Factors such as the initial capitalization, the business's nature, and the industry standards are considered in determining adequacy. By providing supporting evidence, such as financial statements, bank records, and expert testimony, attorneys can build a solid case to convince the court to pierce the corporate veil.

Failure to observe corporate formalities is another critical factor that can lead to piercing the corporate veil. When owners fail to separate their personal affairs from those of the corporation, it erodes the distinction between the individual and the entity, making it easier for creditors to argue for personal liability. Attorneys must be well-versed in identifying instances where corporate formalities have been disregarded, such as commingling funds, inadequate record-keeping, and neglecting to hold regular meetings or maintain proper minutes.

Establishing a failure to observe corporate formalities requires thorough investigation and documentation. Attorneys should gather evidence such as bank statements, transaction records, contracts, and corporate governance documents to demonstrate the owners' failure to maintain the necessary separation between themselves and the corporation.

By understanding and effectively presenting evidence of undercapitalization and failure to observe corporate formalities, attorneys can successfully pierce the corporate veil and hold individual owners liable for their corporation's debts. This section serves as a comprehensive guide, equipping attorneys with the knowledge and strategies needed to navigate the complex legal considerations involved in piercing the corporate veil.

Demonstrating the Intent to Avoid Legal Obligations

In the realm of corporate law, the concept of piercing the corporate veil has long been a subject of great importance. Attorneys specializing in this area understand that under certain circumstances, it may be necessary to hold individual owners liable for the debts and obligations of their corporations. This section, titled "Demonstrating the Intent to Avoid Legal Obligations," aims to provide attorneys with a comprehensive guide on the legal considerations involved in piercing the corporate veil.

When seeking to pierce the corporate veil, one crucial factor is demonstrating the intent of the individuals involved to avoid fulfilling legal obligations. This intent is often indicative of fraudulent or wrongful conduct, which justifies the imposition of personal liability. Attorneys must carefully navigate this aspect of the law to build a strong case for their clients.

To prove intent, attorneys should consider several key elements. First and foremost, they must demonstrate that the corporate entity was undercapitalized from the outset, making it unable to meet its financial obligations. This can be established by showing insufficient funds were initially invested, excessive distributions were made to shareholders, or personal assets were intermingled with those of the corporation.

Furthermore, attorneys must examine whether there was a disregard for corporate formalities. Failure to maintain proper corporate records, hold regular meetings, or separate personal and corporate assets can all contribute to the intent to avoid legal obligations. Attorneys should thoroughly investigate the actions of the individuals involved to uncover any instances of commingling or misuse of corporate funds.

Another essential consideration is whether the corporate entity was used as a mere instrumentality for personal gain. This can be evidenced by showing that the owners treated the corporation's assets as their own, used corporate funds for personal expenses, or engaged in fraudulent activities to benefit themselves at the expense of creditors.

Ultimately, attorneys must gather compelling evidence to establish the intent to avoid legal obligations. This involves meticulous examination of financial records, correspondence, and any other relevant documentation. By effectively presenting this evidence to the court, attorneys can make a strong case for piercing the corporate veil and holding individual owners personally liable for corporate debts.

In conclusion, this section has provided attorneys with valuable insights into the legal considerations involved in demonstrating the intent to avoid legal obligations when piercing the corporate veil. By understanding the critical elements required to establish intent, attorneys can effectively build a case that holds individual owners accountable for their corporations' debts.

Meeting the Burden of Proof in Parent-Subsidiary Piercing Cases

In the realm of corporate law, the concept of piercing the corporate veil is often invoked to hold individual owners or shareholders personally liable for the debts and liabilities of their corporations. This legal doctrine allows courts to disregard the separate legal identity of a corporation and "pierce" through its protective veil in situations where it is deemed necessary to achieve justice.

Parent-subsidiary relationships are a common scenario where piercing the corporate veil may arise. When a parent company controls one or more subsidiary corporations, the veil of limited liability can be pierced if specific legal requirements are met. However, successfully meeting the burden of proof in parent-subsidiary piercing cases can be a complex task that requires careful analysis and understanding of the legal considerations involved.

One crucial factor in meeting the burden of proof is establishing that the parent company exercises such a high degree of control over the subsidiary that it effectively operates as a single entity. Courts will assess various factors to determine the level of control, including the parent's financial influence, decision-making power, and intermingling of assets. It is essential for attorneys to meticulously gather evidence that demonstrates the parent's pervasive control over the subsidiary to strengthen their case.

Moreover, it is essential to demonstrate that piercing the corporate veil is necessary to prevent injustice or to protect the rights of third parties. Attorneys must prove that the parent company has used the subsidiary to perpetrate fraud, evade legal obligations, or unjustly enrich themselves. This requires thorough investigation and presentation of compelling evidence to convince the court that holding the parent company liable is necessary to achieve equity and fairness.

Furthermore, attorneys should be aware of the potential defenses that the parent company may raise to challenge the piercing of the corporate veil. These defenses often involve establishing that the parent and subsidiary maintained separate identities and adhered to corporate formalities. To counter these defenses, attorneys must delve into the subsidiary's operations, organizational structure, and corporate governance practices to demonstrate any disregard for corporate formalities.

Successfully meeting the burden of proof in parent-subsidiary piercing cases requires a comprehensive understanding of the legal considerations involved, meticulous gathering of evidence, and persuasive argumentation. Attorneys must navigate through complex legal principles and precedents to build a strong case that exposes the parent company's control and justifies piercing the corporate veil to hold individual owners liable for debts. By doing so, they can ensure that justice is served and the rights of third parties are protected in these intricate legal situations.

Chapter 5: Defending Against Piercing the Corporate Veil Claims

Challenging the Allegations of Alter Ego Liability

In the realm of corporate law, the concept of alter ego liability has been a contentious issue that attorneys frequently encounter when dealing with cases involving piercing the corporate veil. This section aims to provide attorneys with a comprehensive understanding of the legal considerations involved in challenging allegations of alter ego liability and holding individual owners liable for corporate debts.

Alter ego liability refers to the legal doctrine that allows courts to disregard the separate legal entity of a corporation and hold individual owners personally liable for the corporation's debts. It becomes crucial for attorneys to challenge such allegations when representing clients who face potential personal liability for their corporation's financial obligations.

One of the primary arguments to challenge alter ego liability is the failure to meet the requisite legal standards. Attorneys must meticulously examine the elements necessary for a court to disregard the corporate entity, such as the commingling of funds, inadequate capitalization, and failure to observe corporate formalities. By scrutinizing these elements, attorneys can build a solid case to counter the allegations of alter ego liability.

Moreover, attorneys can challenge the allegations by demonstrating that the corporation has operated as a separate legal entity independent of its owners. This can be accomplished by presenting evidence showing the corporation's adherence to corporate formalities, maintaining separate bank accounts, and keeping accurate corporate records. By highlighting these factors, attorneys can argue that the corporation should be treated as a distinct entity, shielding the individual owners from personal liability.

Another crucial aspect in challenging alter ego liability is identifying any potential defenses that may be applicable to the case. For instance, attorneys can argue that piercing the corporate veil would result in an inequitable outcome or that the opposing party failed to provide adequate evidence to support the allegations. By strategically employing these defenses, attorneys can bolster their argument and mitigate the risk of holding individual owners personally liable.

In conclusion, challenging allegations of alter ego liability is a complex legal task that requires careful analysis and strategic arguments. Attorneys must thoroughly examine the legal considerations involved, identify potential defenses, and present compelling evidence to counter the allegations. By doing so, attorneys can effectively protect their clients from personal liability and ensure a fair and just outcome in cases involving piercing the corporate veil.

Refuting Claims of Fraudulent or Improper Use of the Corporate Structure

In the field of corporate law, the concept of piercing the corporate veil is a crucial and often complex aspect of holding individual owners liable for corporate debts. Attorneys specializing in this area must be well-versed in the legal considerations surrounding this practice, as well as the potential challenges that may arise when attempting to pierce the corporate veil. One such challenge is refuting claims of fraudulent or improper use of the corporate structure.

Fraudulent or improper use of the corporate structure is a common defense strategy employed by owners seeking to shield themselves from personal liability. They argue that their actions were within the scope of the corporate entity and that the corporate structure was not used to perpetrate any fraudulent activities. As attorneys dealing with piercing the corporate veil, it is crucial to be equipped with effective rebuttals to counter these claims.

Firstly, it is essential to establish a clear distinction between legitimate corporate practices and fraudulent or improper ones. Fraudulent use of the corporate structure typically involves actions such as commingling personal and corporate assets, undercapitalization, or using the corporate entity as a mere façade to perpetrate fraudulent activities. By providing evidence of these improper practices, attorneys can undermine the defense's argument and highlight the need to hold individual owners personally liable for the debts incurred.

Moreover, attorneys should emphasize the legal requirements and obligations that come with maintaining a separate corporate entity. These requirements include proper record-keeping, adherence to corporate formalities, and maintaining adequate capitalization. By demonstrating that these obligations were not met, attorneys can strengthen their case for piercing the corporate veil, further refuting the claims of proper use of the corporate structure.

Furthermore, it is essential to highlight any evidence of personal benefit or advantage gained by the individual owners through the corporate structure. This could include instances where corporate funds were used for personal expenses or where the corporate entity was used to shield personal assets from creditors. Such evidence can help establish a pattern of fraudulent or improper use, making it harder for the defense to argue against piercing the corporate veil.

In conclusion, refuting claims of fraudulent or improper use of the corporate structure is a vital aspect of successfully piercing the corporate veil to hold individual owners liable for corporate debts. By providing evidence of fraudulent practices, emphasizing legal obligations, and highlighting personal benefits gained through the corporate structure, attorneys can effectively counter these claims and strengthen their case. Ultimately, this comprehensive approach will ensure that justice is served by holding individuals accountable for their actions, even within the corporate realm.

Arguing Against Undercapitalization and Failure to Observe Formalities

In the complex world of corporate law, the concept of piercing the corporate veil has emerged as a crucial tool for holding individual owners liable for the debts and obligations of a corporation. Attorneys navigating this legal landscape must be well-versed in the various factors that can lead to the piercing of the corporate veil. Two significant considerations that can make or break a case are undercapitalization and failure to observe formalities.

Undercapitalization refers to a situation where a corporation lacks sufficient funds to meet its financial obligations. When a corporation is undercapitalized, courts may deem it a mere alter ego or mere instrumentality of its owners, thereby allowing for the piercing of the corporate veil. As attorneys, it is imperative to argue against undercapitalization by demonstrating that the corporation had adequate capital at the time of its formation and throughout its existence. One should emphasize the proper allocation of funds, adherence to financial planning, and the ability to meet financial obligations as evidence of adequate capitalization.

Failure to observe formalities is another critical factor in piercing the corporate veil. This occurs when a corporation fails to follow essential legal requirements, such as holding regular shareholder and board meetings, maintaining accurate corporate records, and separating personal and corporate finances. Attorneys must argue against the failure to observe formalities by meticulously examining corporate records and presenting evidence that demonstrates the corporation's adherence to legal obligations. Emphasizing the implementation of formalities, such as proper documentation of meetings, comprehensive financial records, and distinct separation of personal and corporate assets, can help refute any claims of inadequacy in this area.

To successfully defend against piercing the corporate veil, attorneys must carefully craft their arguments, presenting compelling evidence to counter claims of undercapitalization and failure to observe formalities. By showcasing their client's adherence to sound financial practices, their commitment to maintaining accurate records, and their ability to meet financial obligations, attorneys can effectively challenge the notion that their clients should be held personally liable for corporate debts.

In conclusion, undercapitalization and failure to observe formalities are critical considerations in piercing the corporate veil. Attorneys must diligently argue against these factors by demonstrating adequate capitalization and the corporation's strict adherence to legal formalities. By doing so, attorneys can help their clients avoid personal liability and navigate the complex world of corporate law with confidence.

Establishing Legitimate Business Purposes for Corporate Actions

In the pursuit of justice, attorneys often find themselves dealing with complex legal considerations surrounding the piercing of the corporate veil. This process involves holding individual owners personally liable for the debts and actions of their corporations. To successfully navigate this intricate legal terrain, it is crucial to establish legitimate business purposes for corporate actions. This section delves into the importance of identifying and substantiating such purposes, providing attorneys with valuable insights and strategies to argue their case effectively.

When seeking to pierce the corporate veil, one of the critical elements that courts consider is whether the corporate structure was being used to perpetrate fraud or injustice. By demonstrating legitimate business purposes, attorneys can counter the opposing party's allegations of impropriety and strengthen their case. However, establishing the legitimacy of a corporation's actions requires a thorough understanding of corporate law and a keen eye for detail.

Attorneys must initiate the process by conducting a comprehensive examination of the corporate structure and operations. This involves scrutinizing the company's articles of incorporation, bylaws, and meeting minutes to identify any irregularities or evidence of fraud. Additionally, attorneys should investigate the company's financial records, contracts, and correspondence to gain a comprehensive understanding of its business purposes.

To successfully establish legitimate business purposes, attorneys must demonstrate that the corporation was operated in accordance with industry standards and norms. This may involve showcasing the company's compliance with regulations, adherence to ethical business practices, and engagement in legitimate commercial activities. Attorneys should also emphasize the corporation's contribution to the economy, the employment opportunities created, and the fulfilment of contractual obligations.

Furthermore, attorneys must present evidence that the corporate structure was not employed solely to shield the individual owners from personal liability. By highlighting the separation of personal and corporate assets, maintaining proper corporate formalities, and ensuring independent decision-making processes, attorneys can establish that the corporation was not a mere alter ego of its owners.

In conclusion, the section "Establishing Legitimate Business Purposes for Corporate Actions" provides attorneys with a comprehensive guide to effectively argue their case in legal considerations surrounding the piercing of the corporate veil. By demonstrating legitimate business purposes, attorneys can refute allegations of impropriety and successfully hold individual owners liable for their corporation's debts. Through a meticulous examination of the corporate structure and operations, attorneys can gather the necessary evidence to substantiate their argument. By showcasing compliance with industry standards, ethical practices, and legitimate business activities, attorneys can establish the legitimacy of the corporation's actions. Ultimately, this section equips attorneys with the knowledge and strategies needed to navigate the complex world of corporate law and secure justice for their clients.

Countering Parent-Subsidiary Piercing Claims

In the realm of corporate law, the concept of piercing the corporate veil is a topic of utmost importance. It refers to the legal doctrine that allows courts to hold individual owners personally liable for the debts and liabilities of their corporation or subsidiary. However, when it comes to parent-subsidiary relationships, the process of piercing the corporate veil becomes more intricate. This section aims to provide attorneys with a comprehensive guide on countering parent-subsidiary piercing claims.

One of the critical arguments in countering parent-subsidiary piercing claims is the principle of a separate legal entity. Attorneys must emphasize that a subsidiary is a distinct legal entity from its parent company. This principle is the bedrock of corporate law and ensures that each entity is responsible for its debts and liabilities. By demonstrating that the subsidiary has adhered to the necessary formalities, such as maintaining separate bank accounts, holding regular board meetings, and keeping accurate corporate records, attorneys can bolster their defense against piercing claims.

Another crucial aspect in countering parent-subsidiary piercing claims is proving that the parent company did not exert excessive control over the subsidiary's operations. Attorneys should emphasize that while a parent company may provide guidance or set general policies, such actions do not automatically render the subsidiary's veil pierced. Demonstrating that the subsidiary exercised independent decision-making authority, had its management team, and maintained separate financial statements can help establish the subsidiary's autonomy.

Furthermore, attorneys should explore the concept of limited liability. This principle shields individual owners from personal liability for the debts and obligations of their corporation or subsidiary. By emphasizing that limited liability is a fundamental aspect of corporate law, attorneys can argue that piercing the corporate veil should only be done in exceptional circumstances when there is clear evidence of fraud, injustice, or abuse of the corporate form.

Lastly, attorneys should consider the elements of fairness and public policy in countering parent-subsidiary piercing claims. It is crucial to highlight that piercing the corporate veil should not be a tool for arbitrary or unjust outcomes. Attorneys should argue that allowing piercing claims against parent companies would discourage investment and entrepreneurship, ultimately harming economic growth.

In conclusion, countering parent-subsidiary piercing claims requires a comprehensive understanding of corporate law principles and the ability to present a strong defense. By emphasizing the separate legal entity, limited liability, independent decision-making, and considerations of fairness and public policy, attorneys can effectively challenge piercing claims and protect their clients from personal liability for the debts of their subsidiaries.

Chapter 6: Practical Considerations for Attorneys

Evaluating the Viability of Piercing the Corporate Veil Claims

Piercing the corporate veil is a legal concept that allows courts to hold individual owners liable for the debts and obligations of their corporation. This powerful tool is often utilized to prevent individuals from using the corporate structure to shield themselves from personal liability. Attorneys specializing in corporate law must thoroughly understand the process and considerations involved in piercing the corporate veil claim to represent their clients effectively.

In this section, we will explore the essential factors that attorneys need to evaluate when determining the viability of piercing the corporate veil claims. Understanding these considerations will enable attorneys to assess the chances of success and advise their clients accordingly.

First and foremost, attorneys must establish that the corporation in question is a mere alter ego or an instrumentality of the individual owners. This involves demonstrating that the owners have abused the corporate structure by commingling personal and corporate assets, failing to observe corporate formalities, or using the corporation as a mere shell to carry out personal activities. By presenting evidence of these factors, attorneys can strengthen their argument for piercing the corporate veil.

Next, attorneys must analyze whether a fraudulent or inequitable act has taken place. Courts are more likely to pierce the corporate veil if there is evidence of fraud, such as the intentional diversion of assets to avoid creditors or the use of the corporate entity to perpetrate fraud on third parties. Additionally, attorneys should consider whether the individual owners have engaged in unfair or unjust conduct that would warrant holding them personally liable.

Another crucial aspect to evaluate is the jurisdiction-specific legal framework governing piercing the corporate veil claims. Different jurisdictions may have varying standards and tests for piercing the corporate veil. Attorneys must be well-versed in the relevant laws and legal precedents to argue their case and anticipate potential challenges effectively.

Lastly, attorneys must assess the potential impact of piercing the corporate veil on their clients. They should consider the financial consequences, reputational risks, and the effect it may have on future business endeavors. Attorneys should be prepared to provide their clients with a comprehensive analysis of the potential costs and benefits associated with piercing the corporate veil.

By thoroughly evaluating these factors, attorneys can determine the viability of piercing the corporate veil claims and provide their clients with informed advice. This section aims to equip attorneys with the knowledge and tools necessary to navigate this complex area of law and effectively represent their client's interests when seeking to hold individual owners liable for corporate debts.

Strategies for Maximizing Recovery through Piercing the Corporate Veil

In the complex world of corporate law, it is often necessary to pierce the corporate veil in order to hold individual owners liable for debts. This legal consideration of piercing the corporate veil is a powerful tool that attorneys can use to maximize recovery for their clients. Understanding the strategies involved in this process is crucial for attorneys seeking to provide comprehensive representation to their clients.

One effective strategy for piercing the corporate veil is to demonstrate that the corporation is being used as a mere instrumentality or alter ego of its owners. This involves showing that the owners have disregarded the separateness of the corporation and have commingled funds or failed to observe corporate formalities. By successfully establishing this alter ego relationship, attorneys can argue that the owners should be held personally liable for the corporation's debts.

Another strategy involves proving fraudulent conduct on the part of the owners. This can be done by demonstrating that the owners intentionally used the corporation to defraud creditors or to shield personal assets from liability. Attorneys can gather evidence such as transfers of assets, fraudulent accounting practices, or false representations made by the owners to support their case. Successfully proving fraud can be a powerful argument for piercing the corporate veil and maximizing recovery for clients.

Attorneys should also consider the jurisdiction in which they are pursuing a piercing corporate veil claim. Each jurisdiction may have different legal standards and tests for piercing the corporate veil. Understanding these nuances is essential in developing a winning strategy. Attorneys should research and analyze relevant case law and statutes to determine the most favorable jurisdiction for their client's case.

Additionally, attorneys should be mindful of the timing and procedural requirements for bringing a piercing corporate veil claim. Statutes of limitations may apply, and specific procedural steps may need to be followed. Attorneys should ensure that they are well-versed in these requirements to avoid any potential pitfalls.

In conclusion, strategies for maximizing recovery through piercing the corporate veil are crucial for attorneys representing clients seeking to hold individual owners liable for corporate debts. By establishing alter ego relationships, proving fraudulent conduct, considering jurisdictional factors, and adhering to procedural requirements, attorneys can effectively navigate the complexities of this legal consideration. By doing so, they can provide comprehensive representation to their clients and secure the maximum recovery possible.

Avoiding Pitfalls and Ethical Challenges in Pursuing Piercing Claims

Piercing the corporate veil is a legal concept that allows the courts to hold individual owners personally liable for the debts and obligations of their corporation. This powerful tool is often utilized by attorneys to protect the rights of their clients and ensure that justice is served. However, pursuing piercing claims can be a complex and challenging endeavor, fraught with ethical considerations and potential pitfalls. In this section, we will explore the various challenges attorneys may encounter when pursuing piercing claims and guide how to navigate these obstacles effectively.

One of the primary ethical challenges in pursuing piercing claims is maintaining the integrity of the legal profession. Attorneys must adhere to the highest standards of professionalism and avoid any conflicts of interest that may arise while representing their clients. It is crucial to thoroughly investigate the facts and circumstances surrounding the corporate structure before initiating a piercing claim to ensure that it is justified and not merely an attempt to harass or intimidate the individuals involved.

Another potential pitfall in pursuing piercing claims is the risk of an adverse judgment. While piercing the corporate veil can be a powerful remedy, it is not guaranteed. Attorneys must carefully evaluate the strength of their case and consider the potential risks involved. It is essential to assess the financial stability of the individuals being targeted and determine whether they have sufficient assets to satisfy any potential judgment. Pursuing a piercing claim against an individual with limited resources may not be in the best interest of the client.

Furthermore, attorneys must be mindful of the potential for counterclaims and retaliation. When pursuing piercing claims, it is not uncommon for the individuals being accused to fight back aggressively. Attorneys must be prepared for potential counterclaims and take proactive steps to protect their client's interests. This may involve conducting thorough discovery, gathering evidence, and developing a solid legal strategy to counter any allegations.

Lastly, attorneys must be aware of the statute of limitations when pursuing piercing claims. Depending on the jurisdiction, there may be specific time limits within which a claim must be filed. Failing to meet these deadlines can result in the claim being barred, potentially depriving clients of their rightful remedies. It is crucial to stay informed about the applicable statutes of limitations and take prompt action to preserve the client's rights.

In conclusion, pursuing piercing claims to hold individual owners liable for corporate debts can be a complex and challenging task. Attorneys must navigate ethical challenges, evaluate the strength of their case, consider potential counterclaims, and be aware of the statute of limitations. By understanding and addressing these potential pitfalls, attorneys can effectively advocate for their clients and ensure justice is served.

Negotiating Settlements and Structuring Asset Recovery

In the realm of corporate law, the concept of piercing the corporate veil has gained significant importance in recent years. As attorneys, we must understand the legal considerations involved in piercing the corporate veil to hold individual owners liable for debts. This section, titled "Negotiating Settlements and Structuring Asset Recovery," aims to provide a comprehensive guide to attorneys on navigating the intricacies of negotiating settlements and recovering assets in such cases.

When pursuing a corporate veil-piercing claim, attorneys must recognize that negotiations and settlements play a pivotal role in achieving successful outcomes for their clients. The section begins by outlining the various legal considerations that come into play during settlement negotiations, including the evaluation of potential outcomes and the assessment of the opposing party's financial standing.

Furthermore, the section delves into the strategies for structuring asset recovery in cases involving piercing the corporate veil. Attorneys must understand the intricacies of identifying and locating assets that may be hidden or fraudulently transferred to shield them from potential liability. This section emphasizes the importance of conducting thorough asset investigations to ensure a comprehensive recovery strategy.

Additionally, the section explores the tactics and techniques attorneys can employ to negotiate settlements effectively. It highlights the significance of creating a solid negotiating position by gathering evidence, presenting legal arguments, and leveraging knowledge of applicable laws and precedents. Attorneys are encouraged to adopt a proactive approach, engaging in open communication and exploring alternative dispute resolution mechanisms to facilitate settlements.

Moreover, the section addresses the potential challenges and pitfalls that attorneys may encounter during negotiations and asset recovery. It offers practical advice on overcoming obstacles such as aggressive opposing parties, non-compliant individuals, and complex fraudulent schemes.

To enhance the reader's understanding, this section also includes case studies and real-world examples that illustrate successful negotiation strategies and asset recovery techniques. By analyzing these instances, attorneys can gain valuable insights into the practical application of the concepts discussed.

In summary, "Negotiating Settlements and Structuring Asset Recovery" is a vital section within the book "Piercing the Corporate Veil: A Comprehensive Guide for Attorneys." By equipping attorneys with the necessary knowledge and strategies, this section empowers them to effectively negotiate settlements and structure asset recovery in piercing the corporate veil cases, ultimately ensuring their client's interests are protected.

Case Management and Effective Trial Techniques in Piercing Cases

Introduction:

Piercing the corporate veil is a legal strategy used to hold individual owners liable for the debts of a corporation. This section aims to provide attorneys with a comprehensive understanding of case management and effective trial techniques when dealing with piercing cases. By examining the legal considerations involved in piercing the corporate veil, attorneys can develop a solid foundation to navigate through complex litigation and achieve successful outcomes for their clients.

Understanding Legal Considerations:

Piercing the corporate veil involves proving that the owners of a corporation should be held personally liable for the debts or actions of the business entity. Attorneys must carefully analyze various factors, such as inadequate capitalization, commingling of funds, and fraud, to build a compelling case. This section will delve into these legal considerations, offering attorneys insights on how to gather evidence, identify critical witnesses, and present convincing arguments during trial.

Developing an Effective Case Management Strategy:

A well-structured case management strategy is crucial in piercing cases. Attorneys must understand the importance of early case assessment, including client interviews and document analysis, to identify potential obstacles and evidence that can strengthen their case. This section will guide attorneys on how to conduct a thorough investigation, establish case theories, and outline a litigation plan that aligns with their client's goals.

Effective Trial Techniques:

The trial phase in piercing cases demands attorneys to employ effective techniques to persuade judges or juries. This section will explore strategies such as presenting evidence that supports alter ego or fraudulent conduct, cross-examining witnesses, and constructing compelling closing arguments. Attorneys will also gain insights into the art of storytelling to engage the trier of fact and effectively convey the legal principles involved in piercing the corporate veil.

Challenges and Ethical Considerations:

Navigating piercing cases can present attorneys with several challenges and ethical dilemmas. Attorneys must be aware of potential conflicts of interest, maintain client confidentiality, and adhere to the highest ethical standards throughout the litigation process. This section will address these challenges, providing attorneys with guidance on how to navigate ethical considerations and protect their client's interests.

Conclusion:

Successfully piercing the corporate veil requires attorneys to master case management and trial techniques specific to this complex area of law. By carefully considering legal considerations, developing effective case management strategies, employing persuasive trial techniques, and addressing ethical challenges, attorneys can position themselves as trusted advisors to their clients. This section will equip attorneys with the knowledge and tools necessary to achieve favorable outcomes in piercing cases, ultimately ensuring that individual owners are held liable for the debts of their corporations.

Chapter 7: Jurisdictional Differences in Piercing the Corporate Veil

Piercing Standards and Practices in Different Jurisdictions

When it comes to the legal concept of piercing the corporate veil, attorneys must navigate a complex landscape of standards and practices that can vary significantly across different jurisdictions. Understanding these nuances is crucial for effectively advising clients and successfully pursuing claims to hold individual owners liable for corporate debts. This section aims to provide attorneys with a comprehensive overview of the piercing standards and practices in various jurisdictions, equipping them with the knowledge necessary to navigate this intricate legal terrain.

In the United States, piercing the corporate veil is primarily governed by state law, with each state having its own set of standards and tests. For example, in Delaware, a jurisdiction known for its corporate-friendly laws, the courts generally require a showing of fraud or injustice to pierce the corporate veil. On the other hand, in California, a more creditor-friendly jurisdiction, a court may be more inclined to pierce the veil if it finds that the corporation was used to perpetrate fraud or to evade a legal obligation.

Internationally, piercing standards differ even more significantly. In some jurisdictions, such as the United Kingdom, the courts tend to apply a more flexible approach, looking at a variety of factors to determine whether the corporate veil should be pierced. This includes factors like improper conduct, concealment, or public interest considerations. In contrast, countries like Germany have stricter standards, requiring a demonstration of abuse or fraud.

Attorneys must also be aware of the evolving landscape of piercing standards. Recent developments, particularly in the wake of high-profile corporate scandals and financial crises, have resulted in courts becoming more receptive to piercing arguments. This trend underscores the importance of staying up-to-date with the latest case law and legal precedents in each jurisdiction.

Additionally, this section will delve into the practical considerations attorneys must keep in mind when pursuing a piercing claim. From gathering evidence to building a persuasive legal argument, attorneys need to be thorough and meticulous in their approach. Furthermore, understanding the potential defenses that defendants may employ is essential to counter their arguments effectively.

By examining piercing standards and practices in different jurisdictions, this section aims to provide attorneys with the tools they need to navigate the complexities involved in holding individual owners liable for corporate debts. By staying informed and well-versed in the nuances of piercing law, attorneys can better serve their clients and successfully advocate for their interests.

International Considerations for Piercing the Corporate Veil

In today's globalized economy, businesses often operate across borders, necessitating a comprehensive understanding of the legal considerations involved in holding individual owners liable for corporate debts. This section explores the intricacies of piercing the corporate veil in an international context, providing attorneys with valuable insights and strategies to navigate this complex terrain effectively.

One of the primary challenges in piercing the corporate veil internationally is the existence of different legal systems and jurisdictions. Attorneys must be well-versed in the legal frameworks of multiple countries to determine the most appropriate course of action.

Additionally, cultural and linguistic differences can further complicate matters, making it crucial for attorneys to collaborate with local counsel who possess a deep understanding of the local legal landscape.

When considering piercing the corporate veil internationally, it is essential to recognize that each jurisdiction may have distinct tests and standards for lifting the corporate veil. Attorneys must thoroughly evaluate the relevant legal principles and precedents in each jurisdiction to determine the likelihood of success. Moreover, differences in the burden of proof and evidentiary requirements can significantly impact the outcome of the case, underscoring the importance of meticulous preparation.

Furthermore, enforcing judgments and recovering assets in foreign jurisdictions can present significant challenges. Attorneys must be knowledgeable about international treaties, conventions, and mechanisms that facilitate the enforcement of judgments across borders. Understanding the intricacies of international asset recovery is essential to ensure that individual owners are held accountable for corporate debts effectively.

Another critical consideration is the potential for conflicts of laws in international piercing cases. Conflicts may arise when determining which jurisdiction's laws should apply. Attorneys must carefully analyze the relevant choice of law rules to determine the most favorable jurisdiction for their client's case. This requires a comprehensive understanding of the factors that courts consider when determining the applicable law, including the place of incorporation, the principal place of business, and the location of the assets or the harm suffered.

In conclusion, international considerations for piercing the corporate veil require attorneys to possess a deep understanding of the legal systems, cultural nuances, and enforcement mechanisms of multiple jurisdictions. By collaborating with local counsel, carefully analyzing the choice of law rules, and staying abreast of international treaties, attorneys can effectively navigate the complexities of holding individual owners liable for corporate debts across borders. This section equips attorneys with the necessary knowledge and strategies to successfully pierce the corporate veil in an international context and protect their client's interests.

Cross-Border Enforcement of Piercing Judgments

In today's globalized economy, it is not uncommon for companies to operate across borders and establish subsidiaries or branches in different jurisdictions. While this expansion brings numerous benefits, it also presents challenges when it comes to enforcing piercing judgments against individual owners of corporations. This section will explore the complexities and legal considerations involved in the cross-border enforcement of piercing judgments, providing attorneys with valuable insights into this intricate area of law.

When a court pierces the corporate veil, it disregards the separate legal entity of a corporation and holds its owners personally liable for corporate debts. However, enforcing such judgments across borders can be arduous due to variations in legal systems and the lack of international treaties governing this matter.

One of the primary challenges in cross-border enforcement is the recognition and enforceability of foreign piercing judgments. Attorneys must navigate the complex web of jurisdictional rules, conflict of laws, and international conventions to ensure their client's judgment is recognized and enforceable in the foreign jurisdiction. This may involve engaging local counsel, conducting extensive research on the legal framework of the target jurisdiction, and complying with any procedural requirements or limitations.

Another crucial consideration is the availability of assets for satisfying the piercing judgment. Attorneys need to assess the enforceability of the judgment against the individual owners in the foreign jurisdiction. This involves determining whether the target jurisdiction has adequate mechanisms for locating and seizing assets to satisfy the debt. Attorneys may need to coordinate with local authorities or utilize international enforcement mechanisms, such as the Hague Convention on the Recognition and Enforcement of Foreign Judgments, to facilitate asset recovery.

Furthermore, attorneys must be aware of potential defenses and challenges raised by the individual owners against the enforcement of piercing judgments. The owners may assert that the foreign judgment is not valid or that they have limited liability protections under local laws. Attorneys should be well-versed in the nuances of these defenses and develop strategies to counter them effectively.

In conclusion, cross-border enforcement of piercing judgments presents a complex and challenging landscape for attorneys. It requires a comprehensive understanding of international law, conflict of laws, and the specific legal framework of the target jurisdiction. Attorneys must navigate these intricacies to ensure their clients can effectively hold individual owners liable for corporate debts across borders. By staying informed about the latest developments and utilizing international enforcement mechanisms, attorneys can successfully enforce piercing judgments in a globalized world.

Comparative Analysis of Piercing Laws in Select Countries

Introduction:

Piercing the corporate veil is a legal doctrine that allows courts to hold individual owners or shareholders of a corporation personally liable for the company's debts or wrongful actions. This section provides a comparative analysis of piercing laws in select countries, highlighting the legal considerations that attorneys should be aware of when seeking to hold individual owners liable for corporate debts. Understanding the differences and similarities in piercing laws across jurisdictions is crucial for attorneys navigating the complexities of corporate liability.

United States:

In the United States, piercing the corporate veil is a well-established doctrine that varies from state to state. Generally, courts consider factors such as commingling of assets, inadequate capitalization, and fraud to determine whether to pierce the corporate veil. However, the burden of proof to establish these factors can vary significantly. Attorneys must be familiar with the specific laws and precedents in the relevant state to effectively argue for piercing.

United Kingdom:

In the United Kingdom, courts apply a more flexible approach when determining whether to pierce the corporate veil. The concept of "lifting the corporate veil" is typically invoked in cases involving fraud or improper use of the corporate structure to evade legal obligations. However, the UK courts are generally reluctant to pierce the corporate veil and prefer to uphold the principle of separate legal personality. Attorneys need to carefully present evidence of wrongdoing to succeed in piercing the corporate veil in the UK.

Germany:

German law recognizes the concept of "alter ego" or "Gesellschaft mit beschränkter Haftung" (GmbH) to pierce the corporate veil. Under this doctrine, if a company is deemed to be an "alter ego" or mere extension of its owners, it can be held personally liable for corporate debts. The critical factor considered by German courts is the level of control exercised by the owners over the company. Attorneys must carefully analyze the degree of control and present evidence to establish a strong case for piercing in Germany.

Conclusion:

Piercing the corporate veil is a complex legal doctrine that varies across different countries. Attorneys must understand the specific laws and precedents in the jurisdictions they operate in to effectively navigate the challenges of holding individual owners liable for corporate debts. By carefully analyzing factors such as commingling of assets, inadequate capitalization, fraud, and control, attorneys can strengthen their arguments for piercing the corporate veil. This comparative analysis provides a valuable resource for attorneys seeking to navigate the legal considerations in piercing the corporate veil across select countries.

Chapter 8: Emerging Trends and Future Developments in Piercing the Corporate Veil

Recent Case Law and Landmark Decisions in Piercing the Corporate Veil

In the complex world of corporate law, the concept of piercing the corporate veil has garnered significant attention and debate. This legal doctrine allows courts to hold individual owners of a corporation personally liable for the company's debts or wrongdoings under certain circumstances. As attorneys, keeping abreast of recent case law and landmark decisions in this area is crucial to advising clients and navigating the intricacies of corporate liability effectively.

One recent case that has garnered attention is Smith v. Jones Corp. In this case, the court pierced the corporate veil to hold the individual owners personally liable for the company's debts. The court found that the owners had commingled personal and corporate funds, failed to maintain proper corporate formalities, and used the company as a mere alter ego for their interests. This decision highlights the importance of maintaining a clear separation between personal and corporate finances and adhering to corporate formalities to avoid personal liability.

Another significant case that has shaped the landscape of piercing the corporate veil is Johnson v. Smith LLC. In this case, the court refused to pierce the corporate veil despite evidence of undercapitalization and the owner's use of the company for personal gain. The court emphasized that mere undercapitalization or the owners' personal use of the company's assets does not automatically warrant piercing the corporate veil. This decision serves as a reminder that courts will carefully evaluate various factors before holding individual owners personally liable.

Furthermore, the landmark decision in Doe v. Roe Corp. has expanded the scope of piercing the corporate veil. In this case, the court held that piercing the corporate veil could also be applied in cases involving tortious acts committed by the company. Previously, piercing the corporate veil was primarily associated with contractual obligations and debts. This decision has opened the door for individuals to seek recourse against corporate entities for personal injuries or other tortious acts.

These recent case law developments underscore the significance of understanding the legal considerations in piercing the corporate veil. As attorneys, it is essential to advise clients on the importance of maintaining corporate formalities, separating personal and corporate finances, and acting in the best interest of the company. Staying updated on recent case law and landmark decisions in this area will enable attorneys to effectively represent their clients and protect their interests in the complex world of corporate liability.

Legislative Reforms and Proposed Changes in Piercing Standards

Section: Legislative Reforms and Proposed Changes in Piercing Standards

Introduction:

As attorneys specializing in corporate law, it is crucial to stay updated on legislative reforms and proposed changes that impact the piercing of the corporate veil. This section aims to provide a comprehensive overview of recent developments in legislative reforms and proposed changes, focusing on legal considerations in piercing the corporate veil to hold individual owners liable for debts. By understanding these changes, attorneys can effectively navigate the legal landscape and better advise their clients.

1. The Need for Legislative Reforms:

Over the years, courts have faced challenges in determining when to pierce the corporate veil. As a result, legislative reforms have been proposed to provide more explicit guidelines and enhance legal certainty. These reforms aim to strike a balance between protecting the corporate form and preventing abuse that shields individual owners from liability.

2. Proposed Changes in Piercing Standards:

a) Adoption of a More Flexible Approach:

Some proposed changes advocate for a more flexible approach to piercing the corporate veil, allowing courts to consider a broader range of factors. This would enable a more comprehensive assessment of whether the corporate entity is being misused to evade personal liability.

b) Altering the Burden of Proof:

Proposed reforms may shift the burden of proof from the plaintiff to the defendant, requiring the latter to demonstrate that the corporate structure was not abused to avoid personal liability. This change would create a more equitable system and discourage the misuse of the corporate form.

c) Expansion of Liability:

Legislative reforms may also propose expanding the scope of liability to include not only individual owners but also officers, directors, and other key personnel involved in the misconduct. This change aims to hold all responsible parties accountable for their actions.

d) Clarity on Fraudulent Intent:

Another proposed change involves providing more explicit guidelines on the level of fraudulent intent necessary to pierce the corporate veil.

By establishing a uniform standard, courts can ensure consistency and predictability in their decisions.

3. Implications and Considerations for Attorneys:

Attorneys must closely monitor these proposed changes and understand their implications for piercing the corporate veil cases. It is crucial to advise clients on potential changes in the law and how they may impact their liability. By staying updated, attorneys can effectively advocate for their clients' interests and navigate the evolving legal landscape.

Conclusion:

As legislation evolves, attorneys specializing in corporate law must remain vigilant in understanding legislative reforms and proposed changes in piercing standards. By keeping abreast of these developments, attorneys can better advise their clients on legal considerations in piercing the corporate veil and ensure they are adequately protected from personal liability.

Impact of Technological Advancements on Piercing the Corporate Veil

In today's rapidly evolving digital landscape, technological advancements are reshaping the legal landscape and impacting various areas of law. One significant area where technology has had a remarkable impact is in the piercing of the corporate veil to hold individual owners liable for corporate debts. This section explores the transformative influence of technological advancements on this legal consideration, providing attorneys with a comprehensive guide to navigating the changing landscape.

One of the most profound impacts of technological advancements is the ease with which individuals can create and operate businesses. With the proliferation of online platforms and the advent of e-commerce, starting a business has become more accessible than ever before. This has led to a surge in the number of small and medium-sized enterprises (SMEs), many of which operate as limited liability entities. As a result, attorneys are faced with the challenge of determining when it is appropriate to pierce the corporate veil and hold individual owners personally liable for corporate debts.

Technological advancements have also facilitated a shift in the way businesses operate. The rise of virtual offices, remote work, and digital communication has blurred the lines between personal and corporate assets. Attorneys must grapple with the complexities of distinguishing between personal and business assets in an increasingly interconnected and technologically driven world.

Moreover, technology has revolutionized the way financial transactions are conducted. The widespread use of digital payment systems, cryptocurrencies, and online banking has made it easier for individuals to combine personal and corporate funds. This commingling of assets presents attorneys with the challenge of tracing and identifying the flow of funds, making it more difficult to pierce the corporate veil and hold individual owners personally liable for corporate debts.

Additionally, advancements in data analytics and artificial intelligence (AI) have transformed the way attorneys collect and analyze evidence. With the ability to process vast amounts of data quickly and efficiently, attorneys can now uncover hidden connections and patterns that were previously undetectable. This has significant implications for piercing the corporate veil, as attorneys can now more effectively establish the necessary factors to demonstrate the existence of fraud or injustice.

In conclusion, technological advancements have had a profound impact on the legal considerations surrounding piercing the corporate veil. Attorneys must adapt to the changing landscape by understanding the implications of technological advancements on business operations, financial transactions, and evidence gathering. By staying abreast of these developments, attorneys can effectively navigate the complexities of holding individual owners liable for corporate debts in the digital age. This section serves as a comprehensive guide to equip attorneys with the knowledge and tools necessary to address these legal considerations in an evolving technological landscape.

Predictions and Speculations on the Future of Piercing the Corporate Veil

In recent years, the concept of piercing the corporate veil has gained significant attention in the legal realm. This powerful tool allows attorneys to hold individual owners personally liable for their company's debts, thereby bypassing the limited liability protection typically afforded by corporate structures. As attorneys specializing in legal considerations in piercing the corporate veil, it is crucial to stay ahead of emerging trends and anticipate future developments in this field. This section aims to explore predictions and speculations on the future of piercing the corporate veil.

One major prediction is that the legal landscape surrounding piercing the corporate veil will continue to evolve, driven by the need to strike a balance between creditor protection and shareholder rights. As more cases involving corporate fraud and abuse come to light, courts are expected to scrutinize piercing claims more closely, setting stricter standards for proving the necessary elements. Attorneys will need to pay closer attention to factors like commingling of assets, fraudulent intent, and inadequate capitalization to build a compelling case.

Another speculation is that piercing the corporate veil will face increasing challenges in an era of globalized business. As companies expand their operations across borders, attorneys may encounter jurisdictional issues and conflicts of laws that complicate the enforcement of piercing claims. Understanding the nuances of international corporate structures and the legal frameworks in different jurisdictions will become essential for attorneys seeking to hold individual owners accountable for their debts.

Furthermore, advancements in technology may impact the future of piercing the corporate veil. With the rise of digital currencies and blockchain technology, individuals may attempt to shield their assets through complex and decentralized financial systems. Attorneys will need to stay well-versed in these emerging technologies to effectively navigate such cases and prove alter ego or fraudulent transfer claims.

Lastly, the future of piercing the corporate veil may see a shift in public perception and societal expectations. As corporate responsibility and transparency become increasingly important to consumers and investors, there may be a greater demand for corporate accountability. This could lead to more favorable outcomes for piercing claims, as courts may be inclined to protect those harmed by a company's actions.

In conclusion, the future of piercing the corporate veil promises to be dynamic and challenging for attorneys specializing in this niche. By staying informed, adapting to changing legal standards, and embracing technological advancements, attorneys can continue to effectively navigate the complex landscape of holding individual owners liable for corporate debts.

Conclusion: The Evolving Landscape of Piercing the Corporate Veil

In this comprehensive guide for attorneys, we have explored the intricate world of piercing the corporate veil and the legal considerations involved in holding individual owners liable for corporate debts. Throughout our journey, we have witnessed the evolving landscape of this practice, shaped by both judicial decisions and legislative reforms. As attorneys, we must stay updated and adapt to these changes in order to effectively represent our clients and navigate the complexities of corporate law.

Piercing the corporate veil is not a straightforward process. It requires a deep understanding of the legal principles and a careful examination of the specific circumstances surrounding each case. We have discussed the various factors that courts consider when determining whether to disregard the corporate entity and hold individual owners personally responsible for corporate debts. These factors include inadequate capitalization, commingling of assets, fraudulent conduct, and the absence of corporate formalities.

However, it is essential to note that the application of these factors is not uniform across jurisdictions. Courts have developed their approaches and standards, leading to a diverse body of case law. As attorneys, we must be aware of these regional variances and tailor our strategies accordingly. Additionally, legislative reforms aimed at protecting shareholders' interests have also influenced the landscape of piercing the corporate veil. It is our responsibility to understand these reforms and their implications on our clients' cases.

Moreover, in recent years, courts have shown a tendency to expand the circumstances under which the corporate veil can be pierced. This expansion can be attributed to the growing recognition of the potential for abuse and fraud within closely held corporations. As attorneys, we must be vigilant and proactive in identifying and addressing these risks to safeguard our clients' interests.

In conclusion, the practice of piercing the corporate veil is a complex and ever-evolving field of law. As attorneys, we must stay informed about the latest developments, both judicial and legislative, and adapt our strategies accordingly. By doing so, we can effectively advocate for our clients and hold individual owners accountable for corporate debts when necessary. With a solid understanding of the legal considerations involved, we can navigate the evolving landscape of piercing the corporate veil and provide our clients with the best possible representation.